MOUTHS

MOUTHS

Claire Marie Stancek

NOEMI PRESS
Las Cruces, New Mexico

for Rasheed & for my mom

missed sliced erased wrist
host asked beast boast
desist crust subsist fast
gust frost messed least
just best distaste assist
obsessed dust persist
insist guest rust ghost
outlast based coast tossed
trust spliced blast spiced
disgust infest defaced
thrust iced test mist exist
resist twist interlaced fist
midst most creased lost
request exhaust addressed
haste priced outlast exist
least bust cast dismissed
consist past rest pest
faced lust nest reduced
roost taste heist list cyst
detest fest cost feast

you wanted never to be
    permeable

yet yes   mist enters you
                through
breath as a mood as a live
turning   thing clouding
space
            the space
between brain and eyes
  a spirit
breathing as you breathe
            host

does mist invade by the
ascendance   of some
ill   star   or
movement of
            tides   or is it
more empty   than that

dust frost cyst exhaust taste
crust reduced rust subsist
list rest feast mist messed
crest resist heist vast
creased persist interlaced
lust best defaced fist midst
cost cast thrust tossed bust
fast iced past addressed
lost gust spiced infest
spliced obsessed waste
desist disgust nest missed
fest most blast detest
sliced dismissed based
wrist distaste pest consist
request boast trust roost
asked just must arrest
pressed coast assist host
guest insist ghost faced
erased addressed frost
distaste just rust waste

dismissed must past exhaust
iced dust lost defaced guest
crust spiced cast haste best
persist heist mist insist
consist roost host resist fist
pest ghost crest reduced
most blast tossed addressed
spliced request feast lust
rust outlast detest fast wrist
just asked frost erased trust
rest messed sliced desist
least priced exist taste cyst
subsist thrust based pressed
cost midst ceased fest
disgust coast arrest beast
boast nest missed waste
assist obsessed bust vast
distaste interlaced twist

your skin flushes   cools
        clouds rapidly
                    shape
        reshape

dissolved bearer you

will not   recognize
your own
body   or any

clouds float through you
and you
        will unknow
feelings   once held
essential   as bones
        feel
what   clouds what   air
   itself feels   air unsung
uninvoked   air   empty

iced   twist   exist   must
pressed assist nest disgust
heist past mist haste dust
subsist cast list least lost
infest   defaced   persist
boast   host pest   messed
crest   exhaust   fest   faced
arrest consist must detest
obsessed   erased   guest
midst   spiced   reduced
missed   desist tossed cyst
cost based rest lust insist
thrust fast blast crust bust
fist pissed outlast taste resist
dismissed feast vast creased
asked   interlaced   wrist
sliced list gust faced infest
haste twist beast ghost lust

CONTENTS

I. HUMAN WHAT THIRST COULD DRAIN YOU

Swarm

dull jar   anarchic sound
        essentially conservative pain   a mistake a

revolt turning too into skin & skin
        swarming   warm arm arc   ark

                        nothing & becoming nothing
                  turning too around the   wheels

                    in wheels of tradition   speaks
            by rubbing sound turning in the skull like a thing

that crawled swarm   around
        airborne figure 8's speaks by turning into

open lives   lines for you   for sound
        dull jar   meaning   loitering

           for the length of exhalation flashing into
              nothing & becoming nothing

                 sibilant buzz   moiling
         eddying in minor channels between

us crawling up the side
        of the neck to where a mistake a

pain speaks by rubbing the hairline begins
        as nothing & becoming nothing

                                    around the curvature of the skull
                                        turning too into the throbbing

                                                    presence would introduce
                                    into the sweet orifice and its waxy canal

a presence which turning too exists
            in the paucity of the possible

lands on hands speaks
            by rubbing front feet back feet together

                                            swarm sinks mouths into skin & skin
                                        turns too into nothing & becoming nothing

                                            throbbing pockets   break open
                                                pink pulp yearning too into

swelling into the rupture open
            reflexively as you hear   &

hearing half create   all senses
            turning too obsolete swarm openings   opening

                                            noses and ears and eyes   mouths
                                                with mouths opening mouths

                                                    where no mouths were

Moth

mouthe, mowth, mowthe, moth, moighte.

A destroyer, a parasite, a maggot, a worm.
When nocturnes bleed indelible: insects
attacking. Like, you are living at my expense.
A parasite. A pair. Appear. Hovering: your
flame. // & your flame. Something that eats
away, wastes, something that eats = some
eating thing). Open open gaping. Pits,
Caves, Wells, Lakes, Fens, Bogs, and shades
of death. Entrance to Hell. Engraven &
scraped / you : of a wound, of a sore rotting
& decaying & become moth-eaten. Eat //
babble in the mouths of children. I asked
& you gave utterance to. Your mouth, as in
shut it. Who articulated silently. Formed on
the lips without voicing.

Moth

air made thick with dark   dust   palpable

churning air churning their   currents   a liquid or a movement

between air and liquid   thick moving dust   our mouths

were filled   those of us who had them had them filled   just breathing

dust a glimmer   at first   then a gloam   filling rush

in our wet mouths   dust hardened   like cement   dried in stopped blocks

our heads fell   down with a crack   stones they were always

waiting to become   our eyes   cracked   the mouths   mouths

flooding   air thick moth night   bashing bodies against glass

some arrived   without wings or with   mangled wings

some died   there on the mantle   the mantle

rushing in   gray brown ribbon   of air   smoke air   mantling

everything   lamp shades in quivering liveness

beating and sizzling   against   lightbulbs

smearing   shadows   ceiling in shadows

gray air   smoke air   dust like living   a dust   a living dust

most large moths like the Luna, Polyphemus, and Prometheus do not have mouths

they press   mouthless   faces to the books

                              and the books crumble   into new   language

eaten having eaten this   a language   and this   is what remains this is remains
            this

if there are holes in this   logic   moths made   grey smoke air   who made

came down with dust   child   his skin   blanketed

dust   on dust   and all turn again and when   he trembled the dust

would fall   in a dirty dry shower   onto   books   the floor

I picked him up   shook him   and he disappeared

in a cloud of dust   a cloud into   which my hands also

light no longer light   light no longer   but churning

dust a shadow   moving shadows   made from   moving   made moving

                                        live air   mottling the walls

Those of us who were left   left

Round

after John Clare

Round The Nest A Welcome Guest
                        A Cunning Guest Goes Bye Unnoticed Still
Ive Hunted White Necks High On Mornings Noise
                        No Memry Left Old Feelings Gloaming Strange
My Manhood But A Memory Left
                        And Neighbour Tennant Spell Struck Listens Close
When Jobbling Fingers Lurch To Fill A Hat
                        And Hopeless Hope Hopes On And Meets No End
Ive Nestled Down In Prisons Still And Strange
                        Remember Still And Still Endure Again
To Peep At Five Ink-Spotted Greeny Shells
                        A Hollow Startling Prison Dwelling Noise
Peal On Peal Revising Feelings Still
                        Swee Swee A Buzzing Loud And Long And Loud
A Stranger Guest Ive Clumb With Hook And Pole
                        Fades But Memry Left A Prison Still
A Hissing Noise Assails A Crimpled Guest
                        Ingulphed Ive Nestled Deep In Evenings Down
As Gusts Again Enraptured Wrap The Nest
                        Where Strangers Heels Tramp Speckled Places Past
And Neighbour Meets With Neighbour Unawares
                        But Still And Still Endure Old Feelings Pains
To Old Ones Cries And Crimpled Quaking Breast
                        A Great White Guest Goes Deafening Bye
And Sluthering Down The Knotty Trunk Amazd
                        Revise Old Feelings Weeding Memry Lost
The Place We Occupy Seems All The World
                        A Strange Formed Accident And Stranger Guest

Swarming

Rain days awash in awareness, wet with all that we knew ourselves to be separate from. We rushed in rain's periphery and we acted by its knowledge, until from the ground came the ants, ants in our bed as we slept and in our hair as we continued to dream dreams of the ants. We slept and we slept longer than we had intended, each alarm in succession becoming cars parked side by side, choir of intention. The cop car tailgated us in its own dream, a short space of road and a rounded shoulder, and when we turned into the driveway it lumbered on. Yellow leaves cluster around a black puddle on a black road sprayed by tires. Streetlights shine in the puddle, they shine on the windshield and keep heartbeat time. Ants cluster around everything dying, dying themselves. Everything that decays and everything that holds life they surround and the bustle of their bodies is a buzzing, aura of night thoughts. They cluster around the sleek tin garbage can, they enliven the pages of that book as if all the letters were crowding for air, they fall into a cup of old water on a desk. All the names are gone, just gone. An old woman slouches in a wheelchair and orange sweatsuit, I see all of my sins crawling into the bodies of animals, she says, I see so many beautiful people. Stale air and a yellow windowless room, when the nurse turns the wheelchair she says lift up your feet, lift up your feet and she says I am lifting them. They jostle dead ants with their antennae, they swarm the poison and run off like spokes on a clock. Suddenly the plate stood on hind legs. Suddenly the man is standing on hind legs waving a violin bow in the rain, car lights white and red streaming past him on either side in innumerable beads, rosaries of time and space, and he's shouting because he can't remember where he parked his car, shouting and surely for this too we will be forgiven, surely the music will vindicate us.

Green

down by eaten flocks   by   herds eaten and overnight
lifting dew dry on   on drying backs

"uncut hair of graves"   bloated turf   in the way
green with green with green with green wreath

corpse hair   grows a green thought not
a green the mind thinks

but rather a thought in shade   bearing the cast of that umbrage
disappearing into green   echoing green or darkening

look at this book   fallen onto the floor   pages
bent and splayed   words

sinking like oily   roots down
words   and sinister intentions   sinking

unkindnesses   unremembered and unnameable   lies and elisions
all sinking   into the apartment below and below

into the earth permeating as noxious rootlets
as cankers on the chafing edge of time   the line's

sliding root   even so will   wreath green   grip
unseeing a thousand tiny eyes   upending loam

Honey

Suspended like voices
bubbling up through honey

A hundred jars of held bodies

One filled with wings another with a finger another has a piece of information

The voices by the time they surface
age   their movement through gleamy oil   a slow toil
voices moving so long bodiless their bodies long voiceless
at the bottom of whatever this is

(Bodies at the bottom for years
turned shell invaded by   gold
by   the   still   well   every   cell
charged   with   a   sweet   that
charges   changes   a   welling
sweet   a   drowning   well   and
good   but   not   well)

And would have been travelling upwards still were it not for you   Being here
to hear them   emerge

Sick, but are you sick enough   yet to die in public   on the cement

Because it was attention
the curl of their bodies around the flower and the care of that gesture

Work: the sweetness of work and the uselessness
    ants begin to moil and the bright money dust squirts and tosses on corn tassels
Neonicotinoid, the colorless color

    Are the bodies in the jars or are they   behind them bulbously magnified
    pulled through the brine by twine eyes   twinned you, object

object   While you see them in the jar   they are
        held by it and by you   you   held
  by   the other side   magnified

    your body turns   gold in gold   smear
your voice moves too   slowly through thickness

        A voice parting honey makes honey's surface dance
            bubbling gargling chopping retching shuddering   the surface of honey dances

    The bodies died long ago now it is your turn
    did you think your own attention would be different
        bending over flowers open mouthed taking sweets

Rose

a swollen smell ruptures the spumy vessel   paining edge
rose-like   rose chewing

for would the rose not chew as a smell as   passively as the rose itself is smelled
rose flowers fester on branches and festering fall

and one adhered   here "rose bruise" you diagnosed   sonorous surgeon
rose bloom fell on her hands

together prest fell as light from glass   as stains and stained
and where they fell the petals stayed

amethyst porphyry vermillion   veins flush and flood shallow skin
words to chew up and blow bubbles of   bubbles of this

sudden a rose came like a full-blown thought,
flushing her brow, and in her pained heart

made purple riot   in hale
the unfurling of the page too is a bloom and you

blew it   what fruit is this   smell of flesh and flower
carving at the skins of one another bleeding out   incredible color   flushed twilight

okay splendid garland   lift the petal and hear it spread
from her hand with the soft snapping of spit   bubbles in an old man's mouth

lift the petal and you will see a spreading web and the color of rot
and a little spider spinning spinning

Root

root, rote, rowt, wrote, rout, ruitt, writ.

To cast a spell, esp. a harmful one, effected
by the magical properties of certain
roots. Remember & still : remember.
Bound // beyond law. In the ground,
we turned around around by the snout.
There in muck & marl we formed a
hole by rooting. Dark with damp and
full of roots. To disturb, disarrange.
Where were you searching. Where
kicking or striking forcefully. Up by
the roots. [   ] Died out completely.

Root

tree mouths reach   slow intent while intent remains still

distorted by earthy glut legion   mouths distended

in embodied dark   legion   rifling massy depths

on an alien scale a season a moment a blind blunt plying

in the spongy regions of potentiality

the body   body of water   human what thirst could drain you

mouths of sinewy silence   mood of the whole meal

in the shade of spicy silver leaves

what message did you carry and polish under your tongue

all your life   into   and out of   age

it turned to seawater and seeped into the walls

and now this tree   drinks of it   mouths hanging   open in

heavy bodied dark and monstrous toil

to be   newly monstrous   rooted in   tooth flesh

long and long   drinking the water of you

that is what came   sink now   slower

Wind

wind, wend, went, wand, want, wound.

As a thing devoid of sense or perception, unaffected by what one does to it. A gap, hole, hollow. What breath spoke & what sounded musical instruments : life. Among the supernatural beings what haunted us // [~~angels, demons, fabulous creatures, dragons, griffins~~]. Decay, as it slips in w ruin & rot. Like, the fact that a person is not present // absent. Under twining plants, whose shadows cast hollow bone dice onto the floor before us : a plight, a knot, a braid. Let those of you who wind, take your twisted way. & those of us who wind : make oaths, strong exclamations. Cold air pours from their beaks. To wrap (a corpse) in a shroud : out of breath. Freq. in passive. With immaterial objects.

Wind

Hear the air   weighting   ice air   where
can one turn   but in air through air
Hear it now   weirdly wilted   saplings snapping

It began as   a wind a wind
clapping dead against window panes winding nerves
Only the dead can sleep in electric lament   it said as they slept
dreaming silver spools that wound

scooping shattered limp lunged wound   an old
form of cold   shaping in air   figures who shimmer and fall

Even in our caves   it reached us   through drafts   cracks
its smell   grainy   gray bread   felling the breathers
the young   rushing red   silver clacking trees

Warm

warm, werme, worm, worn, warn.

& you asked what degree of heat is ""natural
to the living organism & what // applied to
tears. Of a kiss, embrace: eager. Like, have
you tasted. Sensation spreading : heat in
the body. I was in the night and night [being
near the object sought] was the person
chosen to seek. Warm with sadness and with
loss. Where conflict carried over, bringing
& bearing // vigorously conducted. Ardent
: full of love : color. If an intimation caught
in time's gross throat. How warm are the
old words. We were denied entry, forbid,
refused. All over & under the slender,
creeping, naked, limbless animal. All among
the serpent, snake, dragon. When grief or
passion preys stealthily.

II. CONSTRUCTION ZONE

Where

after Lisa Robertson

Where have you been, Lord Randal, my son?

A fence of shadows, a shadow fence.

And where have you been, my handsome young man?

A flat blue horizon ruffled with cloud bank.

Over a bluff washed in slime and bright shadows.

A motorcycle mirror reflecting bricks.

Past the weddings of strangers.

A shadow fence elongated under the actual fence.

Over bright waves frothed in foam.

A wall of windows, light on the floor.

Where rooftops connect to other rooftops.

Along a muddy river streaked in slime and floating bottles.

Smell of an old fountain.

Along a river whose surface reflected high buildings, filled all filled with slime and floating bottles.

Past dim storefronts with orange awnings.

Along a steaming sidewalk.

Where have you been, after time, after all this time?

Along ditches filled with lanky flowers.

Up the slit-staired overpass where every step opened the possibility of falling up sun, parted heads, obedient, pharmaceuticals, rounded shoulders, soldiers.

Along streets whose gray grayed the sky.

And where have you been?

Along the shadowy side of the street.

A fence of shadows, a shadow fence.

Along the shadowy side of the street.

Down stairs running under the peeling white paint.

And where have you been?

Down stairs to where the woman in purple watches the tracks.

And where have you been?

Into the train.

And where have you been, my wasted one?

CONSTRUCTION AHEAD

And where have you been, my star-drunk child?

Under the steel bars sectioning sky.

AWARD WINNING HOTDOGS

With a string of orange flags fluttering.

Blue condoms, red condoms, yellow condoms, pink condoms.

Through the airless station.

Buzz of flickering neon.

Past one fizzing and staticky streetlamp, a yellow orb against the still blue sky.

CONSTRUCTION AHEAD

Past a crow huddled into its feathers.

CONSTRUCTION ZONE

Through a tunnel with a ghoulish green light.

Delicious Dips—Scrumptious Salads

Past an open window.

Down stairs running under the peeling white paint.

Under a clocktower.

Down stairs to where the woman in purple watches the tracks.

With a black hat.

Down the glass escalator.

Past a man all in white, biking like a stripe of light.

EROTIC OUTLET

Past a sagged corner where loose garbage bags sat flopped.

Carrying the cup of water to me like a child you said I thought you would find this beautiful, inside was a drowning moth flapping dust against sheer walls of glass.

Smell of clucking brown water.

Her key in the door.

With a cellphone.

Hollow tub drum of empty bottles floating.

EROTIC OUTLET

I am weary.

I am weary.

I thought I did at the time.

Hollow tub drum of empty bottles floating.

Into the screaming train.

A motorcycle mirror reflecting bricks.

Into the station whose windows reflected a more perfect sky: thin racing clouds and the blue, a bird, two, poised high and paused as though in search.

Over a green canal.

Into the station with melting white windows.

Pinging bike bells.

Into the train.

A wall of windows, light on the door.

Into the train.

Along the shadowy side of the street.

Into the train.

Into the train.

NO PARKING

Where five bars of light tell long time.

NO PARKING ANY TIME

Through the smell of water watering the drought.

NOT A THROUGH STREET

I thought I did at the time.

This is all I need in my life.

Through the gate between illuminated green arrows.

Over a bluff blanketed in invading purple.

Under the shining plastic caves holding cameras.

Over a bluff washed in slime and bright shadows.

Past a man in the yellow paisley tie.

Over a green canal.

TURN LEFT

Over a mossy bridge.

Past the massive green eye.

Over bright waves frothed in foam.

Past white concrete walls bearing parallel shadow bars.

Past a column carved with a woman's face.

Through city streets receiving a wet blue night streaked in pink clouds.

Past a crooked dripping pipe.

Past bikes chained against railings.

Past a crow huddled into its feathers.

Past a crooked dripping pipe.

Past a man all in white, biking like a stripe of light.

Past an old couple, bent into their walking.

Past a man in the blue shirt.

SOCIETY SHOP

Past a man in the yellow paisley tie.

Over a mossy bridge.

Past a man on a cellphone talking quickly.

Along a steaming sidewalk.

Past a sagged corner where loose garbage bags sat flopped.

Through a door breaking the sky into a spree of curled steel.

Past an old couple, bent into their walking.

Buzz of flickering neon.

Past an open window.

Where the cathedral sits like a mushroom: swollen and moist, blank and resplendent.

Past bikes chained against railings.

Smell of floating mud.

Past dim storefronts with orange awnings.

Smooth white steel filmed in fine grime.

Past massive succulents spreading star-shaped bundles.

With that song that reminded you of spring.

Past one fizzing and staticky streetlamp, a yellow orb against the still blue sky.

WC

Past railings blurry with spray paint.

With a brown strap over one shoulder.

Past the man in the white hat.

Suck and flap of plastic in the wind.

Past the massive green eye.

Under a tree whose trunk was surrounded by a metal bench.

Past the weddings of strangers, mother make my bed soon.

Past a man on a cellphone talking quickly.

Past two pigeons.

Through a long black tunnel.

Past white concrete walls bearing parallel shadow bars.

With a skinny cat.

Past white concrete walls covered in spray paint, indecipherable messages.

Smell of tires in the sun.

Piercing fall smell of burning.

Past white concrete walls covered in spray paint, indecipherable messages.

Pinging bike bells.

Down the glass escalator.

Smell of an apple in a white plate with cigarettes.

AWARD WINNING HOTDOGS

Smell of an old fountain, cavernous mold.

Through fields that bear a ghostprint of window's glass.

Smell of clucking brown water.

Through rushing tunnels.

Smell of floating mud.

Past railings blurry with spray paint.

Smell of high wind, blue sky, fat clouds.

Her key in the door.

Smell of people walking past, the wall of air they drag behind them.

Where have you been, you, you, you?

Smell of rust in the fog, mother make my bed soon.

Up stairs with rusted blue railings.

Smell of tires in the sun.

Up stairs the same color as the mottled grey sky.

Smooth white steel filmed in fine grime.

Into the screaming train.

SOCIETY SHOP

Smell of an apple in a white plate with cigarettes.

Suck and flap of plastic in the wind.

A flat blue horizon ruffled with cloud bank.

Through a dim tunnel with one wall flickering falling night.

Where glass eventually becomes sky.

Through a door breaking the sky into a spree of curled steel.

Delicious Dips—Scrumptious Salads

Through a door with engraved handles.

A shadow fence elongated under the department of defense.

Through a long black tunnel.

Under the gibbous cameras.

Through a tunnel with a ghoulish green light.

Along a river whose surface reflected high buildings, filled all filled with slime and floating bottles.

Through city streets receiving a wet blue night streaked in pink clouds.

Past a column carved with a woman's face.

Through fields that bear a ghostprint of window's glass.

With wet and trampled paper.

Through low gardens bordered by neat square hedges.

Smell of high wind, blue sky, fat clouds.

Through rushing tunnels.

CONSTRUCTION ZONE

Through the airless station.

Under an open window.

Through the gate between illuminated green arrows.

NOT A THROUGH STREET

Through the hot station.

This is all I need in my life.

Through the smell of water watering the drought.

Under the spotted and streaked ceiling.

TOW AWAY ZONE

Past a man in the blue shirt.

TURN LEFT

Into the train.

Under a clocktower.

Where have you been?

Under a tree whose trunk was surrounded by a metal bench.

Blue condoms, red condoms, yellow condoms, pink condoms.

Under a window with a pink horse pushed halfway through.

Along streets whose gray grayed the sky.

Under an open window.

TOW AWAY ZONE

Under grey mottled skies.

Past massive succulents spreading star-shaped bundles.

Under the gibbous cameras.

Past two pigeons.

Under the shining plastic caves holding cameras.

Piercing fall smell of burning.

Under the stained and streaked ceiling.

With a fine wire connecting two poles.

Under the steel bars sectioning sky.

Over a bluff blanketed in invading purple.

Up stairs the same color as the mottled grey sky.

Along ditches filled with lanky flowers.

Up stairs with rusted blue railings.

Where dancers in a circle bend down and smack the cement.

Up the slit-staired overpass where every step opened the possibility of falling up sun, parted heads, obedient, pharmaceuticals, rounded shoulders, soldiers.

And where have you been, my star-drunk child?

WC

NO PARKING

Where dancers in a circle bend down and smack the cement.

Into the station with melting white windows.

Where bars and pipes cross the ceiling.

Through the hot station.

Where five bars of light tell long time.

Smell of people walking past, the wall of air they drag behind them.

Where glass eventually becomes sky.

Through a dim tunnel with one wall flickering falling night.

Where have you been?

With wires crowding and straggling, a near miss.

Where have you been, after time, after all this time?

Under a window with a pink horse pushed halfway through.

Where have you been, you, you, you?

Smell of rust in the fog.

Where have you been, my son, my son?

With cigarettes.

Where rooftops connect to other rooftops.

Under grey mottled skies.

Where the cathedral sits like a mushroom: swollen and goggled, smooth and sentient.

Through a door with engraved handles.

With a black hat.

Past the man in the white hat.

With a brown strap over one shoulder.

Along a muddy river streaked in slime and floating bottles.

With a cellphone.

Into the station whose windows reflected a more perfect sky: thin racing clouds and the blue, a bird, two, poised high and paused as though in search.

With a fine wire connecting two poles.

Along the shadowy side of the street.

With a skinny cat.

Through low gardens bordered by neat square hedges.

With a string of orange flags fluttering.

NO PARKING ANY TIME

With cigarettes.

With darker clouds joining lighter.

With darker clouds joining lighter.

Where bars and pipes cross the ceiling.

With that song that reminded you of spring.

And where have you been?

With wet and trampled paper.

Carrying the cup of water to me like a child you said I thought you would find this beautiful, inside was a drowning moth flapping dust against sheer walls of glass.

With wires crowding and straggling, a near miss.

III. WHAT IS IT TO HOLD BUT TO ECHO

This living and

Opening her jaws to its jaws the animal ate one more animal. Strange kiss, devouring. A crash brought two strangers together for the length of one car was crunched, a flowering of metal. The uncontrollable shaking began as a handshake, but that hand, so warm and capable, wouldn't let me go, and now I carry it and its seething seizing wherever I walk and dream. Capped waves capped by a bottom, a bottomless hunger. The way your brother cried as if four babies were crying at once. The way your baby drank from your body as if you had the answer. A voice hears you but doesn't speak, although the runes molder, although you need that voice. When the moon waxes, three of us remember. In the old times, these bodies knew the motions and the motions were voices in the swollen moon. All the time the animals knew exactly what you did to them. The feeling of that hand crowds and clamors with the other feelings—with the feeling of cold, and of blue, and the feeling of *and*—and sometimes squeezes out all but the sensation of fingertips rasping and asking and asking the alien skins, the calfskins cracked and thumbed dry, thrummed tuneless. Querying in the chambers and the galleries, where the ghost limbs still hover and vaguely ache, reaching perpetually from those dead words.

Hold

after Drake

a.

How many times can you remember the face before it becomes your own face

         voice before   your own voice

What is it to hold but to echo

b.

this is the only sound you should fear

& what home when   on the border of this black lake rimmed with light

home when waiting we hear singing from
deep inside the lake, singing as though the force of night itself were calling out

if home were a sound
where or in which
time returns   sound inside of

                                                    sound and in turning   /
                                                    return:

Time return, time return

just hold on

c.

Let us hold everything that ruin left us

Let us offer, let us, let us

Let us adhere here

Let us grasp and let us take

Let us bear and in bearing, hold

Let us subsist and let us hold true

Let us keep keep keep keep

Let us agree and let us be held

Let us reserve and let us hold

Let us hold everything and let everything wait

Let us comfort and let us cling

Let us endure together and sustain

Let us reserve it all including time, including enough time

Let us hold and together delay

Let us restrain the chord and with it, let time itself be restrained

Let us believe and let us hold

Let us hold this, and this too

Let us depend and let us belong

Let us hold our breath

Let us hold back and hold forth

Let us own it, own it, own it

Let us hold and let us be held

Let us hold that chord

Let us occupy

Let us hold up and let us hold on

Let us be capacious and let us be possessed

Let us hold together and wait

Shade

after Keats

When the shade of the tree fell
                                    came a ruin
on the walkers
                                    light and shade
on the wanderers whose motion defined
                                    some other Body—the Sun
regions of warmth hand from heart
                                    relish of the dark
from ground and warmed the ground
                                    in whose soul
                                    night's labours should be burnt
when this shade pressed the skin
                                    even the finest Spirits
of the walkers they were seized
                                    in a very little time annihilated
by the coolness of the shade and by its unusual
                                    character in whose soul
sweetness which parted the mealy air
                                    some other Body
like a marauding silver spirit
                                    lives in gusto
the walkers became enfolded in shadow
                                    no Identity no nature
rooted and from then on only moved as shadow
                                    speculating on creations
moves elongating with the sun
                                    not itself no self
gathering dark in calmed fingers

Living Stones

In arid air living stones sleep. Sleep is a word standing in for another mode, one that exceeds logic and the shape of thought, and the leggy boundaries of its own name; a consciousness not of time or of the span of day, but of sun as a space that opens a little room onto the conditions of being, sun as a space into which being opens, slowly, more slowly than any sentence that opens on its own time, fold upon fold, and sometimes perhaps folding back upon itself, a reaching being rummaging for life in the atria and arcades of its heart; more slowly than any movement that might be discerned by the eye, even the most patient eye, returning with the day to illuminate the same words on the same page and to watch for any sign from them, any shivering or shimmering or even the softest shifting that might betray a sympathy towards the questions which lie writhing; more slowly than the passing of a life through all the stages of gestation and senility, and even more slowly than thoughts themselves travel, as they echo from life to life and bind together in ghostly symmetry the ages. The touch of sand against the skin of the living rock is this sleep's dream, a million fingers on the breeze, a community of smells or tastes, a language mixed with memory and the desire only for more sleep.

Fray

after CHVRCHES

read dregs　　/　　what was made　　/　　impervious

　　stains the wall　　/　　hook print　　/　　said

forbidden　　/　　bade forebode　　/　　*every human touch*

　　will be replayed　　/　　restrain shade　　/　　retrograde

Egg

out of chaos grew shape before shape grew out of chaos
emerging from the chaunt of dreams

a presence blank as the expectation born of a rhythm begun
weave the night denser and denser with dreams

what dream out of chaos the bright egg warms waiting
the wires in your voice obscure you with music

what dream out of chaos waits warm in the world
wind, wind in the leaves becomes wind in the crate

the bright yard divides in black diamonds of mesh wire
the wings press the wire press the feathers press the wings

Repetition

after Purity Ring

I look for signs that unruly time has looped its tangle

You: pregnant in grey cloth

You: on the phone at work

One hand suspended

Your eyes reading air to the rhythm of what you hear

Let us be skies strewn incredibly at dusk

A wall of windows reflects what glare remains

Watching the fire take your eyes

If under the proposition lay a coiled wire its edges live and streaming

What transmittance might emotion wreak

Kept time kept out

In the pane hangs a face shaped like a face staring back

Web

★

hunger a pose of pure intent
poised on hunger
poisoned hanging, a wait
pure hunger purifying
holding the body in tense
poison pose, hunger pure
what do you propose if
anything
live in hunger hunting

★

*Long is the list of
supposed negative traits:
over-ambitious projects,
dexterity, cunning,
ambition, ruthlessness,
avarice, poisonousness.*

★

light weaving light waiting
light on light silken weight
taste of blood, the sweetest light

★ what smell   the smell of blood

★

*It has always been admired for its intricate filigree structure, and for the fact that it is both
a way to gather sensory information and, when needed, a skilful instrument of capture and
entanglement. The fact that it is spun out according to semi-abstract designs from the body
of the spider, that it can sometimes be recycled and used anew, can serve as a*

★

*but in the same breath might
represent—given the frailty of the
web—the mindless effort of work,
and perhaps its pointlessness*

★

filigree firmament:
look at the lines
parting sky from sky

★ *she fills the Air*

⭐

Long is the list of supposed
negative traits: over-ambitious
projects, dexterity, cunning,
ambition, ruthlessness, avarice,
poisonousness.

⭐

And this Empyreal substance cannot fail,

⭐ *she*

⭐

longing light

⭐ ruddy blood the hectic
spice

⭐ *Major ampullate silk is the rope spiders depend on as they*
plunge

⭐

It is one of the toughest materials on earth, able to withstand great
stress and absorb immense amounts of energy without rupturing.

And until platinum filaments and improved glass engraving replaced
them in the latter part of the twentieth century, major ampullate ⭐
threads made ideal crosshairs for surveyors' transits, telescopes, and aware in air
other optical instruments. of air as air
itself is, for air
is, but not how
you think
pendant lattice
turn, turn

★

she fills the Air with a beautiful circuiting

★

Long is the list

★

the soul in our body exists exactly like a spider in his net. She cannot move without vibrating one of the widely strung threads, in the same way as one cannot touch one of the threads without setting the spider in motion

★

*over-ambient process,
dis/misclarity, stunning
ambrosial luminance, madness,
ominousness.*

★

*But the Minds of Mortals
are so different and bent
on such diverse Journeys
that it may at first
appear impossible for any
common taste
and fellowship to exist*

★ *And this Empyreal substance
cannot fail,*

★

knowing shapes as smell only
ruddy blood the hectic spice
insects and dream bodies
massy forms in the night

Mural Breach

after Alice Munro

How wet the earth and how wilde

flat brick brink   remembering how mumbling and mute the time before

the sun throws itself in vibrant violence across

How unquenchable the earth and how dark

flat bricks wrench out dreams
in their dreams wrench out

                                  drone

                              wilde capt

                                      cloud capt towers,   foam
                               the gorgeous palaces

                                      clap to the heart   moan
                      falling in the dream the bricks dreamed

direction down

volley sound and sun
          the yearning of stones that hear

return return

How erroneous the earth and how unquenchable

the dust of falling rubble rises   and in the dust a dream receives

F

after Lil Wayne

1

We tried to feed the mouths but the mouths fed us
We drank at their teeth   how in speaking they swayed

In a dream a million mouths danced   they turned and in turning became wings
Suspended   between the end of one sound and the beginning of another

Wings became feet and feet became frenzied and frenzy became form

form was fever, a fever of wings
and the f is for

                                                                future

2

not sick   but ill

You're a feast you're a fog   fragment meant   increment
    firmament
a fiend but   what's a fiend =

        fever blossomed and bore fruit

wings flinging   of f

3

o   f   and the f is for

4

fill (filling a) frack (forming a) flood (flooding a) fetish (feeling a) flout (facing a) feel (fishing a) flock (faking a) fault (forcing a) fright (fucking a) flow (forgiving a) fume (freezing a) flash (fretting a) flavor

Move

after Miley Cyrus

But were we even together said air to air, guest in the sound,
even on that day? On the blurred blue neon bridge where
the others were blurs on black background, but were we
together? Or now, in midst of dance dance dance. Propose,
put forward, say, solicit. Before a black glassed wall where our
bodies are flattened and returned all shine and dim glimmer.
Move in movement and be moved. Excite, arouse, stir up.
On the street where your voice was seagull scream, car horn,
sidewalk mist exhalation, a click shut, a question, whir of
wings, a braced ring-ring of iron grids walked on. To bow
in acknowledgement or salutation. *And a Britney song was
on*, where were you on the internet that day? Because the
tree branches were in the wires rustling together and their
shadows below showed little difference between life and live.
Of a voice or part: to proceed from note to note. To con-
trol, govern, like the way the curl of iron braces sky, though
the clouds passing through that frame actually aren't. Host
in the station for a moment passing through a sign that says
many dimensions. Where a pattern of bricks falling up over
tree roots bunching under. Permeable to sound, guest and
a host. Every particle in welcome to the movement enters
through the enters through the sound. Find a buyer or be
sold. Approach with the purpose of attacking. And were we
even together of something mechanical? To proceed away
from a place where one is considered by a police officer to
have stood too long. To go from one place, position, state, to
another. And superimposed, the bright silhouette enters
open enter.

Pond

falling cold rain in the black sky turns grey white

joining the water the water falls into

grey white the cold rain in warm water shaping

into the water the water falls into

cold like a shape in the body of pond

trembling the surface the raindrops make tremble

come come murmurs pond water turning to meet you

into the sound of the sky meeting water

come come murmur shapes in the body of sound

joining the sound of the sky meeting sound

two bodies join in the turning cold body

cleaving the pond like a spill the cold fills it

two bodies one in the body of pond

cold like a shape like a cloud in the pond

turn turn murmurs rain water rushing the black sky

into the pond like a cloud the cold spills in

soon soon says the pond in an opening turn

into the surface between sky and water

into the surface whose circles are sound

Higher

after Rihanna

I remember light streaks
surfaces, our

atmospheres,
see also listening, hear

what is unnameable
aura that arose within reception, the way

I'm feeling magnifies that
which you take

into consideration
you know, by thinking, you know

by sensing
from the balcony, this goes as far

and as fast as possible, a hundred
sources at once, *you*

take me higher

SATURATED BY EVENING, HALF LIGHT

Mouth

So this is how history eats
choke the garble *do you*
Please

words   through   a
festering egg
Come in, Come in

We are a small language
Side by side   side   side

words   waiting
shadow because   must be
known   and you do
understand them
You do, you do, you

By the rules of courtesy, of
grammar, by the demands of
response
Come in

And what new things, and
invade, and what hard things,
and what opening
Invade

Thank you
Please

And eat, please
Falter in the face

language do you begin
    with   which sounds in
your dreams
Always a guess

In the mouths of calling children,
listen to the listen
breaking through
Come in

So is how history eats, so this
is how
Slow, a melting slow, slow
carve

These words, these sounds
      break palate
pellets   hard volumes
flat swellings
Do you, do you, you do

The forgetting has begun
      begun
In the voices of children

Watch the slow mouthing,
watch one eating

The tyranny of
comprehension

We are a small language
folded into the continent, into
the consonant
How warm are the old words,
crumbling comfort

Must be known, these words
please, please
Come in

And the head turns, and with
it the mouth, and with the
mouth, the open
Come in, Come in

Open breaking sound
open multiplying mouth
Thank you

half light

꙳

In a dream, all the handles were hands, some squirming some grasping, some with spindly fingers, some spiked with nails. Open the door and come in. A dream of the end, of after the end, the end: a door held fast, hands locked, hands stopped. After the end, these wrought hands remain as echoes, echoes of echoes they made on a door knocking. Open the door and come in. Times between sleeping and waking when language pushes through, physical world shudders and blooms, a tree all shivering leaves and sky, my hand reached a handle, *I hold it towards you.* Times between sleeping and dying dreams come back, as though the world of dreams were a dropped basket with frayed ribbons gone streaming, or is it just the way the light hits: cerulean, chartreuse, coral. *Pink granite shows splinters of light which are its ecstasies.* I dreamt of a door with hand handles, and years later, in the train, an old woman said that my hair reminded her of her mother's, argent, ash, mist, and she pressed this photo into my hand:

Keats

Etel Adnan

you say you hear human voices / but they're only echoes   Arcade Fire

✸

half light   entropy of night
   on the phone   smudges   your voice   moon

mad flight mad   flight   stars strobes streetlights   bodies
half night

and saw a circle of demons   dancing
and   danced   among   myself   demon   legion

your love will set you free   Caribou

✸

an echo   a ghost   a mood   an exhalation

✸

In the half light, light emanates from things themselves, radiates
electric, a buzzy taut brilliance, trees and glittering leaves, they shiv-
er the air. In the half light, a brief time opens, a time in which signs
proliferate: cobwebs wobbling inside a black wrought iron gate,
their fur snarling afternoon light, dreamy glow; a small witch with
a green face hanging suspended from a string; a fridge, at a crooked
angle, by the curb. Like, *I am among // limbed elms / colluding with*   Julian Talamantez
doves, like, —*dusk, an improvisation: a chaos/ritual*—   Brolaski
                                                                         Julie Carr

✳

a name resurfaces   lives   later
    an image   chemical bath dark   cat   room   comes running

haunches   trembling   sidewalk   drops   cipher, what   rune *her*   Tonya Foster
self is a sleep

    from another life: a red boat, a book, some volumes of ghost
stories, *translated from the German into French, fell into our hands.*   Mary Shelley

✳

where live brother the times my
brother willow remember mud do you
remember breath damp spring snow mud cattails the invention

of language yes you say yes but your sidewalk eyes don't
remember it that way invention
of language in your hand your phone our reflections

peeling backwards in warped
angle from glossy cars our reflections flash gone
glossy cars in the willow drought remember yes but I can hear

the year fading in the half light

✳

Like, *Officer, I heard the sound of the sun / and it meant burn them down*   Jane Gregory
Like, *But these are my hands. But the sun burns my hands. Kill the sun.*   Bhanu Kapil

✺

what remains

        embody, you call   it   *smells like*   *ghosts, it*   Aase Berg
           smells of slop
                flesh,

what of these our ephemera

✺

How will our voices echo after after   Brandon
not a ghost / but a man of ash without speech   memories move   Shimoda
and live in the shadowy realms of music, half-phrases
of songs and their moods,
moods roam alongside songs, echoes too

not a phrase whole, but in pieces *I also told you: live by night.*   Etel Adnan

＊

Drake says, *mixing vodka and emotions / tapping into your emotions / dry cry cause I'm hopeless.* Rhyming emotions with emotions like emotions mixing, as though the force of repetition itself could perform the jolt at contact of one person's emotions tapping into and mixing with another person's. *Calling of name sound, turned.* Repetition both stalls and spurs the sequence. Two words touch, their sameness setting off their difference.

Myung Mi Kim

＊

your love will set you free you love your will set free set your free will you love set free you will your love you set free will your love will your love set you free free love will set your you love your set you free will your free will you set love your free will you love set set your love you will free love set will free your you you your love set free will you free love set your will set free you love will your will love set you free your

＊

Maybe this distance isn't even real distance, because the world we've made together is composed of something that is beyond geometry and time, and that's the world that we live in always, whether we are physically near or not.

Rasheed

※

I shall read a passage of Shakspeare every Sunday at ten o' Clock you read
one at the same time, and we shall be as near each other as blind bodies can
be in the same room.   Keats

※

oh oh oh strobe,   to my body
  what
     ephemera   is to thought,   running ahead

  the rest is noise   Jamie xx
    dear dream

were dream   flesh the mind takes
  teeming brain   as in   manifest   as in   blue balloon   Keats

cigarette   a bee's stinger
     between swept slabs, stuck among dust and cat hair
empathy and love   Gabriel
  are not enough   Gudding

※

Like, *strange how the half light / can make a place new / you can't*   Arcade Fire
recognize me / and I can't recognize you
Like, *it seems like the only time you see me / is when you turn your*
head to the side and look at me differently   Drake

70

※

Crows cough outside the window, cold air pours from their beaks
all over my skin, which becomes thick with goosebumps. *Through*
me flew a bird. The sky is grey slate. You text and say you're crying
and hyperventilating in bed and need to cancel our date.

Jalal Toufic

※

     in the half light
          of my jealous heart !   *I cried*

Purity Ring

   until my bodyache

Purity Ring, kenning across
     grammar   cracking
            verb into noun (tooth smacking kiss):

                (em)brace(d)

In Drake's song "Redemption," a three-line progression moves
and stays the same:

> I know you're seeing someone that loves you
> and I don't want you to see no one else
> I don't want you here with no one else
> I don't wanna do this with no one else

Mantras fossilize feelings on whose brittle support motions and
habits weigh and wear

No one else becomes a promise, attains the force of promise, it
rises / through repetition and we hear it as heartbeat, the promise
heartbeat makes / *No one else*

❉

I propose that the sound of poetry is heard in the way a promise is heard. A Susan Stewart
promise is an action made in speech, in the sense not of something scripted
or repeatable but of something that "happens," that "occurs" as an event
and can be continually called on, called to mind, in the unfolding present.
When I promise, I create an expectation, an obligation, and a necessary
condition for closure. Whether we are in the presence of each other or not,
the promise exists. Whether you, the one who receives the promise, continue
to exist or not, the promise exists. Others may discontinue making and
fulfilling promises, the word promise might disappear, you or others may no
longer remember, or deserve, or make sense of that promise—nevertheless,
the promise exists.

❉

The etymology of promise is from the Latin verb *promittere*, "send
forth; let go; foretell; assure beforehand, promise." Coiled now,
radiating future but impervious to it. Future, after all, only echoes
promise. More than prophecy which predicts, the promise asserts,
whether or not it is fulfilled.

I am ephemera in the face of my promises. A negative from
another life *fell into our hands.*

I am the man on the left, calling out to the black sky, which was a sky strained pale orange, saturated by evening, half light :   this negative echoes falsely after its promise, which was the unrememberable actual sky that night : and o ! its   sweet   incandescent smell

✹

ghost of the ghost of the lyric: a mirror grey with dust

ghost of the ghost :

     Sometimes I see nothing in the cemetery   Allison Cobb

after you and I are gone   after the   end   of human life
let these   dreams   seethe   still

Adam said that when Drake says, *I gave your nickname to someone else*, it's not an example of erasure but rather of honoring a memory, even to the point of obsession. Beloved ghost. *something about the music the music / curls up in boxes* And repetition again intervenes in time. *Please give me time*, Drake repeats in the refrain, *cause I'm searching for these words / to say to you*

Fred Moten

The repetition makes time and wastes time. Time sticks on the line, running forwards and backwards, a *subway. boxcar. cable car. street car. trolley. tractor. bulldozer.*

Bernadette Mayer

Please give me time
It's the same argument as Milton makes in his sonnet, "When I consider how my light is spent"—

Ere half my days, in this dark world and wide

Is standing and waiting what repetition is trying to effect? A way outside speed and time? Both Drake and Milton linger on the line ends, dragging the line on and asking it to be longer—Drake through repetition, and Milton through enjambment. Even still, it's time that poets beg for. Time and light / in the half light

⁂

    with what voice does an echo speak
and with what voice

drive your car on the bones of the dead, through cities strangely   Sina Queryas
    deserted, under overpasses shaking

with train weight   corridor   of columned shadows : half light
like / How voices are the bodies of words   Shane McCrae

in sidewalk chalk, blue   blurry with dew, I could barely read
    only at certain times in your life will you be alive

⁂

Now if this is so, is it not possible—I often wonder—that things we have   Virgina
felt with great intensity have an existence independent of our minds; are in Woolf
fact still in existence? And if so, will it not be possible, in time, that some
device will be invented by which we can tap them? . . . I feel that strong
emotion must leave its trace; and it is only a question of discovering how
we can get ourselves again attached to it, so that we shall be able to live
our lives through from the start.

⁂

sky strewn with pale blue pebble clouds, light behind palpably gold
half light

✸

Like the idea that eternal return is about us and our agency, that we can always come back—and if not an exact repetition, with a slight difference, like how I hated leaving the bay but now find myself, all of a sudden, surrounded by AZNs and tacos and pho and weed all over again.

Seulghee

✸

And when all of these emotions run themselves out of repetition, and when our hearts stop mixing and beating and flushing and breaking, after the end of our lives, and after the end of human life, what ephemera remain. Let these dreams seethe still / shadows, half light

✸

Please give me time

And by me, I mean us. And by us I mean: *you, you, you*

In the half light, I look for the difference between promise and curse. Behind one door, the curse, behind the other, the promise. *Your punishment has been prefigured as of old.* I reach for wrought hands, the hands of my dream. *"The" opening "you" put in "them."*

thirteenth-
century curse
Aaron Kunin

For you were mown down in the eucalyptus groves, down snorkeled and flushed by intricate mechanisms through the veined underbelly of the metropolis, and you were reduced to babble in the mouths of children, in children's mouths you burbled, incoherent, cut out from the flesh, from veins, bleeding and weeping and hacking up pus, for you were tangled with the snakes in the dank of the well windows, where the cool earth bred miasma and mushrooms, and you were thrown from the bluff, where you became a diminishing sparkle dissolving into dusk, for you were a toad at the ear of Eve, and in the cries of birds and in the moans of livestock, you exhaled your wet steam, warm with sadness and with loss, for your loss was our loss, and we are lost / half light

Through the power of all the saints you are tormented, crushed, and sent down to eternal flames and underworld shadows

like, *Here's to the dissident apple—olla*

Lyn Hejinian

✸

Cecil Giscombe

A miracle's an   impulse,
      "an impulsive act"; a story trails

  its own noise.   demon's priest   incants
     echo: a hand   a fold   a line of flight   a flake of glass
Confession

TC Tolbert

is the logical opposite / of light

✸

80

Like, *I am libidinous in my syntax & gluttonous in my forms*
Like, *pressed spiders between a book's pages cure holiness stop*

Cody-Rose
Clevidence
Rusty
Morrison

✸

our fight   slips from   night   into
      the world of dreams my body / rises

      into waking   intervals   *moon juice*   blue   still
      our fight   waits gargoyle   shape   misshapen

Aaron Apps

      bewildered with dreams   they say that *A body*
is forgetful,   but I am thinking

Angel
Dominguez

only of *the orchard the orchard the orchard: the: ocean*

Dominguez

※

When I came home today, *dressed all in black like an omen*, I walked
into the bedroom—and hanging low in the pine trees outside the
window was the most incredible, neon-pink full moon, radiating
with a life and what felt like a direct gaze. I had to blink at it for
a few moments to discern whether it was the moon rising or the
sun setting—and only the coolness on my eyelids as I stared sug-
gested to me that it was the moon. I took some pictures, but they
were pale and white, nothing like the bright pink eye in the sky,
so I won't include them, but in their place will leave these : cool :
moons : of the past   here

Lil' Kim

(Here both recognizes and demands recognition.)

Claudia
Rankine

※

✺

Yet the poet, if he is a poet, does not describe the mere appearance of the sky and earth. The poet calls, in the sights of the sky, that which in its very self-disclosure causes the appearance of that which conceals itself, and indeed as that which conceals itself. In the familiar appearances, the poet calls the alien as that to which the invisible imparts itself in order to remain what it is—unknown.

Heidegger

✺

Like when Daniel says *cosmic fortune*, like when he says *I am thinking that a poem could go on forever*

✺

My own shadow, loopy, lumbery, long, and fuzzy around the edges in the diffuse sunlight, cast in front of me on the sidewalk as I turn the corner onto San Pablo; a couch with battered corners, its cushions upended; intensely bright fuchsia flowers running riot up a house roof; a lithe, spotted grey cat running up to me as though to give me a message, *every poem is a navigational chant*, but then running right past me and ducks into an alleyway, slipping behind garbage dumpsters

Craig Santos Perez

＊

I love 2 Chainz's exuberance of citation, *"sleep is the cousin of death"* / *that is some Nas shit.* In the same spirit I'll say, *"Bluish light surrounds her"* / that is some Mei–Mei Berssenbrugge shit.

＊

Rasheed says that the swallow's flight answers *yes,* that *life inheres*
         outside the parameters   speaks

    with voices of the dead   incantations
   resound as   echo   *Death*

unburdened   nothing / but a tunnel of sunlight   Lynn Xu
        mannequin heads   stubble hair   hacked   *heightened*

perception, which is hauntedness   Elizabeth
                                                                            Robinson

＊

Like, *extinction level event*
Like, *apocalyptic garden is gonna be so fresh*

                                                                            Busta Rhymes
                                                                            Brandon
                                                                            Brown

84

In the half-light, the graffiti'd stone face swells vibrant neon,
shadows linger   rearrange graffiti into doubtful shades
flicker   a mood   wings

I said your name in an empty room   Arcade Fire

Promise

after Virginia Woolf

I propose that the sound of poetry is heard in the way a promise is heard.
                    —Susan Stewart

Now if this is so, is it not possible—I often wonder—that things we have felt with great intensity
have an existence independent of our minds; are in fact still in existence?
                    —*Virginia Woolf*

Sound a calamitous sound concussive in the
waves, a crashing louder than the mile-long waves
it breaks in crashing, *rhythmical, and half conscious*
and like something wrapped in mist, desist desist,
creatures—crustaceans, blooming now madly
blooming jellyfish, fish like little silver fingers
boiling through weeds, and fish like massive minds
that hear for miles and sound out cries for miles in
wavelike song—all flee, flee the sound that fills and
in filling breaks, bursts, opens past bursting and still
burgeons wider *like some vast sucker, some glutinous,*
some adhesive, some insatiable mouth, a sound that
brings blood to the eyes and mind, a sound that
makes the ears go mad, the maddened mottled
ears in miles of flesh gone washing up the beach,
gone breaking with the broken waves on sand—
marine, (*Like a long wave, like a roll of heavy waters,*
he went over me, his devastating presence—dragging me
open, laying bare the pebbles on the shore of my soul)—
marine, *It is strange that we, who are capable of so much*
suffering, should inflict so much suffering; listen to the
bursting you articulate

(but still a few stars fall through night, beautifully, from the violence of that concussion)

> If ever a sound had power to repeat on its own
> iron throat recoiling, if ever a rhythm could return
> to its own bland and hulking sounder—and may
> I not be misheard in treading the bleeding dark
> of this my curse, our curse, O human—then may
> your sonar wreak itself on you, and may your
> vessels pop and curdle in the fracturing sound,
> and may you wash yourself bloated in black waves

CODA: LET US ADDRESS OURSELVES TO THE CURRENTS

Here

And here lies one who grew wings
And here lies one whose skin became luminous, more luminous than the sun
And here lies one who died drone
Who fell asleep

Aged 6 years, 4 months deeply missed RIP
Forever loved Doctor, wife, mother What remains of us is love

Where lies she who filled her body with sounds
Where lies she whose eyes
And where lies one who was murdered far away
Bore the mark of fingers

In loving memory of In cherished memory of Killed in action near Le Sars, France
So young, so fair, so brave In loving memory of Forever with the

And here lies one who fed madly on the night air and died
And here lies one who died of exhaustion
And here lies the place
Here lies the place

Here lie stones whose bodies contain time beyond time
But where lies the oil, and how deep
And here lies soil soaked with oil
And here lies one   computer, across the world

Family grave in loving memory
God touched him and he slept "I spake as a child"
You live in your children You live in our hearts

We will never forget you in faith and love my devoted husband

Where lies she around whom   pooled
Luminous with poison
Where lies she who held toil in her hands, and who bore weight on her shoulders
Who fell asleep

Who was killed by a message, far away
Who choked on the shadows
Who bathed in the sound of night, in the cool water, and in the echo of these in
the pine woods
Who drank starlight and died

Where lies the oil, and how deep
Here lies a green one, here lies a blue one
Where lies earth dark with damp and full of roots
Where lies the water flowing sweet under earth

A man of men To strive, to seek, to find, and not to yield
Here lie the ashes of my dear husband after 50 years together, never forgotten

Where lies she who weathered
Sadly missed Sweet mother, thank you
Who died of the sound of fingers tapping at the night window
Who seized the sounds in the night with shaking fingers

The righteous shall be in everlasting remembrance
In everloving memory of my darling wife

And here lies one who was killed by another one
Who lived a short life
Whose blood
And here lies one whose cause of death

Wife of the above
Who fell asleep

Whose life was as a storm
Whose fingers knew the sounds of the notes, whose fingers sang the notes
Found, as if by chance, by a computer far away
Who died of the slow fingers curling through the night

Come unto me all ye that labour and are heavy laden and I will give you rest
Who was touched by the hand of God and slept

Garden

Here the people stream, cluster, crouch, holding out cameras

Here the people confer in small groups before dispersing into porous walls

Here the people hope for continued hope

Here more people act in the place of the other people who again were acting in the
        place of the other people before them

Here the people glance sidelong at their reflections in the window

Here the people gesture and nod, turning toward and away from one another

Here the people murmur in vague health, and hope for continued complacency

Here for a moment the amaranths think thoughts that the people had strangled with
        their presence

Here the people collect, holding cameras out to other people

Here the people step back several paces, looking up at the gargoyle

Here the people imagine the garden with no people

Here the people clip by holding smooth leather satchels

Here the people feel less hopeful than they did before

Here the people wish the other people out of the garden

Here the people murmur thanks for hope

Here for a moment, suddenly, the garden is empty of people

Here the people clip by in wingtips, their ties flapping in the open breeze

Here the people avoid including in their photographs the other people taking
        photographs

Here the people collect in clusters, holding cameras against the amaranths, holding
        cameras at arm's length, holding cameras to their faces

Here the people feel inexplicably bereft

Here for a moment the amaranths are transported with thoughts beyond expression,
        thoughts strangled by the presence of the people

Here the people gesture with bags slung over one shoulder

Here, suddenly, one pigeon flaps graceful as a thought across the garden to perch on a
        gargoyle

Here the people feel more hopeful and more forgiving of themselves than they did
    before
Here the people feel more hopeless than before
Here the people feel spiritually realigned
Here the people confer in small groups
Here the people are invaded by a sudden fantasy of a garden without people
Here the people bend in pairs over the placards
Here for a moment the garden is filled with amaranths free suddenly of people
Here the people walk as though unspeakably tired, as though pressed down by an
    exhaustion beyond individual exhaustion
Here the people hold their cameras up
Here more people again hold cameras against amaranths and at arm's length and again
    they hold cameras up against the bushes and step back and point their cam-
    eras at the gargoyled arches and the amaranths together
Here this fountain reproduces itself endlessly in the photographs of the people
Here the people turn toward and away from one another, nodding and bending into
    the placards
Here the people meet the eyes of the people looking at them coolly and coolly look
    away
Here the people step thoughtfully around the fountain before bringing the cameras up
    to their faces
Here the people clasp hands behind their backs, looking up to frown at the gargoyles
Here the people disperse into porous walls as their replacements arrive
Here the people feel hopeful and hope to be more hopeful in the future
Here the people walk with one hand in a pocket
Here the people accidentally meet the eyes of other people and look away
Here the people take three steps back, looking steadily up at the gargoyle before
    bringing the cameras up to their faces
Here the people consider the fountain, and hold their cameras to their faces

Here for a moment the people wait, paused at the porous doorway

Here this fountain manufactures itself endlessly in the same photograph in hundreds of
        cameras

Here the people suddenly wish the other people gone

Here the people are invaded by a sudden fantasy

Here the people feel healthy and realigned, deciding to feel hopeful about the future

Here the people feel healthy and hopeful

Here the people wait for the other people to be finished taking a photograph before
        they step in and take the same photograph

Here the people walk with almost limping steps, slowly

Here for a moment all the people have suddenly left the garden

Here for a moment the amaranths join their colors to the breeze

Here the people linger in the porous doorways

Here for a moment the garden sways

Here for a moment the amaranths nod and sway

Here again the garden is permeated by clusters of people, people holding cameras,
        holding open leaflets, bending over the placards

Sunken

Where the vibrant branches entwine and twist, the uncounted float through
Where are your million million arms twisting in dance

To the currents whose movement rubs out color
Let us address ourselves to the currents

Arms at arm's length right arm the auld moon in her arm
Under the mist in the thickening present, the acid freaks and rubs

Uncounted city and what
And let us address ourselves to the climbing acid

Boulevards shining, of machines, as of a balance
And let our voices be understood by the winnowing gray, the force of death

And what is lost if nothing is known of the arms arm in arm taking arms
Deeds or feats your seething millions

An extraordinarily well-balanced arm
Within scarves of billowing color, the dance dissolves the dance in acid gray

With open
And what is destroyed nothing

Bodies press the crowd where folds enclose the crowding, the bodies that press
and follow, the bodies that make their way and make the currents in their going,
in their pressing, and their being, unreal
Sunken city, where are your seething millions

And where are your scarves folded in a million falling currents, and a million
billowing directions
And what million million ways of being and of moving

Man in arms to arms at arms up in taking bearing under order
Nature having armed him a creature so armed

Great sea, out of which the arme proceedeth
Thickening, taste the forms in brittle change, the force of death

Where are your receding red distances
Sunken city, where are your passageways and secret doors that lead

One speaks in an ancient language and the uncounted follow into twilight arch-
ways and dim imaginings
One dissolves into a billow of long scarves dissolving

Riuer, which runneth into the sea with two armes
Vibrant branches leech to take and to hold

Painted with the movement of movement itself, and when you moved the whole
city turned
Arm-linked and swept, arm-twisted and linked, arm band arm bone

Recede the acid waves having formed him a creature
City, where

City, city, where are your translators
Arme, arme, and out

Acknowledgments

Grateful acknowledgement to the editors of the journals in which these poems first appeared:

Animal: "Moth" (Stephen S. Mills)
Berkeley Poetry Review: "Mouth" and "This living and" (Jules Wood and Rachel Feldman)
Bone Bouquet: "Move" (Krystal Languell)
Cold Cut: "Where" (Perwana Nazif)
Colorado Review: "Green" (Donald Revell and Stephanie G'Schwind)
Cordite: "Web" (Kent MacCarter)
JERRY: "Rose," "Root," "Root," "Wind," "Wind" (Emily Wolahan)
Oversound: "Sunken" (Liz Countryman and Samuel Amadon)
RealPoetik: "Round" (Thibault Raoult)
Room: "Line" (Taryn Hubbard)
Typo: "Honey" (Adam Clay)

Thank you to everyone at Noemi Press, to Carmen Giménez Smith, Sarah Gzemski, Diana Arterian, and to J. Michael Martinez for perceptive editing. Thank you to Emilie Clark for permission to use her painting *Untitled (EHR) 36* from *Sweet Corruptions,* 2012. on the cover, and to Steve Halle for designing the book.

Thank you to the teachers past and present who have challenged and led me, especially to Lyn Hejinian for endless generosity and inspiration; to my dissertation advisers, Kevis Goodman, Elisa Tamarkin, and Ian Duncan, whose insights shape both my academic and creative work; to Rusty Morrison, Cecil Giscombe, Sina Queyras, and Geoffrey G. O'Brien; to Adam Fitzgerald and everyone at the Ashbery Home School; to my first teachers, especially Deidre Lynch, Deirdre Baker, Nick Mount, and Cannon Schmitt; and to my students for their brilliance, with particular thanks to 최 Lindsay, Jacqueline Last, and Perwana Nazif.

Deep, deep thanks to my friends who read and discussed versions of the manuscript: Brandon Brown, Jane Gregory, Serena Le, Seulghee Lee, Christopher Miller, Emily Wolahan, and especially to Daniel Benjamin for reading these poems many times, always with wisdom.

Thank you to my family: to my father, brother, and grandfather McGarity; to my beloved Baba Yaga, Jaroslava Blažková, whose witch blood pulses in these lines; to the Tazudeens, for support and love during the writing of these poems. Thanks, finally, to my mother, whose love, belief, and example of work structure my every day; and to Rasheed Tazudeen, for living and breathing these words with me—this book is for the two of you.

About the Author

Claire Marie Stancek is also the author of *Oil Spell* (Omnidawn, 2018). With Daniel Benjamin, she co-edited *Active Aesthetics: An Anthology of Contemporary Australian Poetry* (Tuumba / Giramondo, 2016), and with Lyn Hejinian and Jane Gregory, she is co-founder and co-editor of Nion Editions. She is currently a PhD candidate in the English Department at the University of California, Berkeley, where she teaches poetry workshops and literature classes. To arrange a class visit, lecture, workshop, or interview, contact her at cm.stancek@gmail.com.